Beanbag Buddies
and
Other Stuffed Toys

Written by Judy Ann Sadler
Illustrated by June Bradford

KIDS CAN PRESS

To my brothers, Richard and Robert,
who are full of beans
and lots of other good stuff.

Published in Canada by
Kids Can Press Ltd.
29 Birch Avenue
Toronto, ON M4V 1E2

Published in the U.S. by
Kids Can Press Ltd.
85 River Rock Drive, Suite 202
Buffalo, NY 14207

Edited by Laurie Wark
Designed by Karen Powers

Printed in Hong Kong by Wing King Tong Co. Ltd.

CM 99 0 9 8 7 6 5 4 3 2 1

Canadian Cataloguing in Publication Data

Sadler, Judy Ann, 1959 –
    Beanbag buddies and other stuffed toys

(Kids can do it)
ISBN 1-55074-590-5

1. Soft toy making – Juvenile literature. 2. Stuffed animals (Toys) – Juvenile literature.
3. Handicraft – Juvenile literature. I. Bradford, June. II. Title. III. Series.

TT174.3.S22 1999   j745.592'4   C99-930069-5

Kids Can Press is a Nelvana company.

Contents

Introduction

What do a sock lion, glove horse, pocket puppy and button bear all have in common? They're all beanbag and stuffed animals you can make. This book begins with easy projects and ends with some that take longer to make. You'll find lists of the things you need, instructions for the stitches and full-sized patterns where necessary to make more than a dozen irresistible animals. Fill them with beans, plastic pellets or soft stuffing to get the look and feel you want. You'll be amazed at how your animals come to life when you fasten the eyes or draw on a lopsided smile. These animals are also terrific for raffles, school bazaars and gifts — that is if you can bear to part with them!

MATERIALS

While you work on these projects be sure to keep needles, pins, scissors and small items such as beans, buttons and beads out of the reach of young children. The finished stuffed or beanbag animals should not be given to babies.

Fabric

There are many different fabrics you can use. Try soft, slightly stretchy fabrics such as velour, sweatshirt fleece and thick, fleecy fabrics such as Polarfleece. You can also use felt, corduroy, flannel and short-haired fun fur or pile. Look for fabric scraps at home, remnants at fabric stores or buy small quantities of the fabric you want. When the instructions refer to the right side of the fabric, this means the good side or the side that shows on your finished animal. The wrong side is usually on the inside where it cannot be seen. Fabrics such as felt and fleece are often the same on both sides.

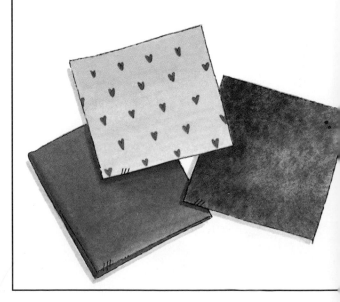

Patterns

Some of the animals require patterns. Trace the patterns from the back pages of this book and cut them out. Glue them onto thin cardboard (such as a cereal box) and cut them out again. This makes it easy to trace the patterns onto fabric and makes them last so you can use them often.

Fabric markers

Use erasable fabric markers to trace patterns onto light-colored fabric. Use a chalk pencil, dressmaker's marker or a sliver of dried soap for darker fabrics. Don't use permanent markers to trace patterns because the ink might show through on the right side of the fabric.

Straight pins

These will hold your fabric pieces together as you sew. Keep them in a small container or pin cushion.

Needles and thread

Use good quality polyester thread that matches your fabric. If you are sewing with thread in fine fabric, use a slender needle with a small eye. For thread in heavy or thick fabric, you will need a larger, sturdier needle. Whenever you sew with yarn or embroidery floss, use a needle with a large eye. You will need a long, strong dollmaker's needle for the sock bunny. You may want to wear a thimble to protect your finger when using thick fabric.

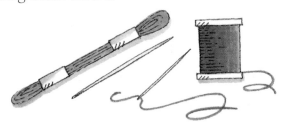

Stuffing and beans

For the beanbag animals you can use plastic stuffing pellets (available at craft supply stores) or dried beans and peas, popcorn kernels or rice. (Make sure your stitches are very small if you use rice.) Don't get the animals wet if they have beans, peas, corn or rice in them. If you are stuffing the animals, use polyester fiber stuffing, clean cut-up rags or pantyhose. Or try a combination of stuffing and beans.

Basic sewing stitches

As you are making your stuffed animals, refer to these pages whenever you need sewing information.

Threading a needle

Cut a piece of thread about twice the length of your arm. Wet one end in your mouth and poke it through the eye of the needle. Or, use a needle threader by poking the wire loop into the eye, dropping the thread into the wire loop and pulling the wire and thread back through the eye. For yarn, tightly pinch a yarn end between your index finger and thumb. Push down into the yarn with the eye of a large needle, threading the yarn into the eye.

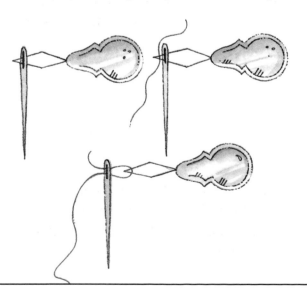

Knotting the thread

Double the thread so the ends are even. Lick your index finger and wind the thread ends around it once. Hold the thread with your thumb and roll it off your finger. Hold the ends and pull tightly to make a knot.

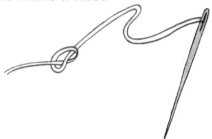

Running stitch

1. With knotted thread in your needle, poke the needle up through your fabric. Poke it back down in a little way over from where it just came out.

2. Keep bringing the needle up and then back down through the fabric. Make the stitches and spaces even and not too tight.

3. When you run out of thread or reach the end, make two or three small stitches on or near the last stitch and cut the thread.

Overcast stitch

1. With knotted thread in your needle, pull the needle through the fabric.

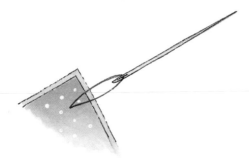

2. Bring the needle around the edge of the fabric and go in again from the same side as the first stitch, but a little way over. Keep stitching like this.

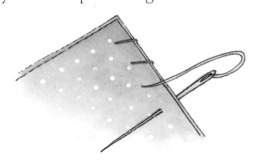

3. When you run out of thread or reach the end, make two or three small stitches on or near the last stitch and cut the thread.

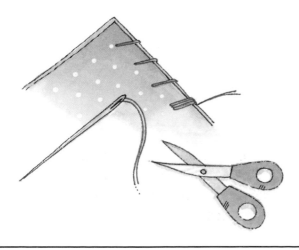

Backstitch

If you have a sewing machine, it can be used anywhere the instructions call for the backstitch. Always ask an adult to help you with a sewing machine.

1. With doubled, knotted thread in your needle, bring the needle up through the fabric about 0.5 cm (¼ in.) from the edge.

2. Poke the needle down through the fabric closer to the edge, then back up a short distance from the first stitch.

3. Poke the needle back down through the fabric at the same spot where you first poked the needle into the fabric. Keep the stitches small, even and close to the edge of the fabric.

4. When you run out of thread or reach the end, make two or three small stitches on or near the last stitch and cut the thread.

Felt friend

Have you ever drawn an animal you wish you could bring to life? Here's a way to do it. Use light- or bright-colored felt so that you can add details with a permanent marker.

YOU WILL NEED

- 2 squares of felt
- a black or dark-colored permanent fabric marker
- straight pins • scissors
- yarn or embroidery floss and a yarn needle
- stuffing • white craft glue
- decorating supplies (see step 8)

1 Use the marker to draw an animal on one of the felt squares. If you'd prefer, you can draw on paper first, cut it out and trace it onto the felt.

2 Pin this felt square on top of the other one. Place the pins around and inside your drawing, but not across the lines.

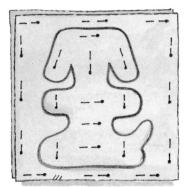

3 Cut out your animal through both layers. Leave any pins that are in the animal, but remove pins from the scraps.

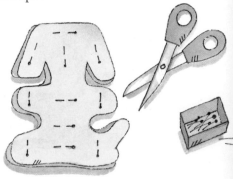

4 If you'd like your stitches to show, use colorful floss or yarn. If you don't, use yarn or floss that matches your felt. Thread an arm's length of yarn or floss into your needle so the ends are uneven. Knot the longer end.

5 Place the needle between the layers of felt and poke it through the top layer. Bring the needle around to the back and poke it through both layers to the front. Continue with this overcast stitch (see page 7) until you are almost back to where you began.

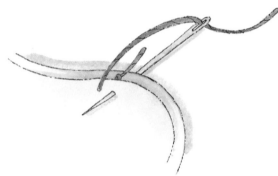

6 Remove all the pins. Push stuffing into all areas of your animal.

7 Sew the rest of the way around. When you reach the end, make a couple of stitches on the same spot and trim the yarn.

8 Add a button or pom-pom nose, bead, rhinestone or roly eyes and a yarn or felt mouth. Use the fabric marker to draw on freckles and paws. Does your animal need a scarf? Whiskers? Big white teeth? A long braided tail?

Painted turtle

A plain, stretchy glove can be transformed into this colorful painted turtle.

1 Knot a doubled length of thread and sew a running stitch around the cuff as shown. Leave the needle and thread hanging.

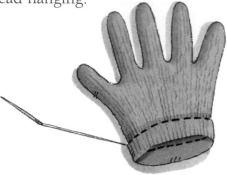

2 Stuff the fingers and thumb. Fold the cuff into the glove and stuff the palm area.

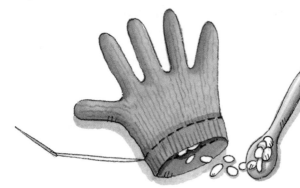

3 Pull tightly on the needle and thread to close the glove and change the position of the thumb. Stitch across the opening to sew it closed. Don't cut the thread.

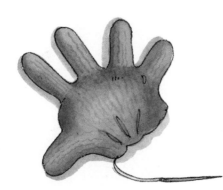

4 Pull the baby finger and thumb toward the gathered area to get a turtle shape and stitch them there. Knot and trim the thread.

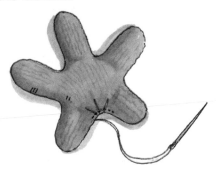

5 Draw an oval turtle-shell pattern onto the thin cardboard and cut it out. Trace it twice on the felt and cut out the two felt shapes.

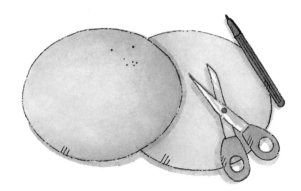

6 Use fabric paint to draw patterns on one or both shell shapes. Also, draw a face and claws on the turtle. Allow everything to dry.

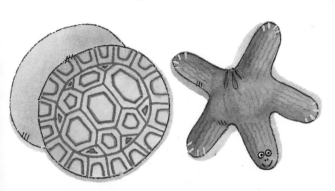

7 Cut out a long, thin felt tail. If you decorate it with paint, allow it to dry. Stitch it to the turtle's body.

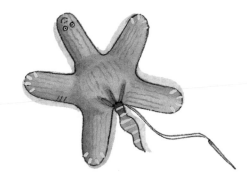

8 Place the turtle between the shell shapes. Stitch the shells together at the sides and on each side of the tail.

OTHER IDEAS

Make the turtle shell all one color or use a different color for the top and bottom. You can even make a fancy shell by gluing on buttons, beads, sequins or colorful patches of felt.

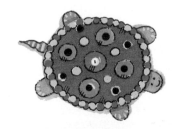

11

Glove horse

After you've made this horse, try other creatures such as a cow with white felt splotches and pipe-cleaner horns, a dalmatian or a dragon with spikes.

YOU WILL NEED

- a needle and thread
- scissors, a ruler and white craft glue
- a stretchy, knit glove
- stuffing or beans   • roly eyes (optional)
- scraps of felt and narrow cord or ribbon
- a large needle and yarn
- dimensional fabric paint

1 Knot a doubled length of thread and sew a running stitch around the cuff. Leave the needle and thread hanging.

2 Stuff the thumb. This will be the head. Fold the cuff down into the glove. Stuff the four fingers and the rest of the glove.

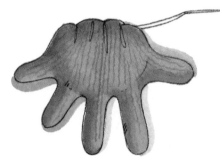

3 Pull tightly on the needle and thread to close the glove and lift the thumb. Stitch the opening closed. Knot and trim the thread.

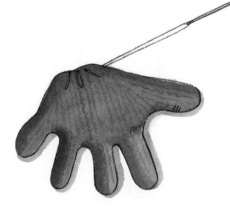

4 To make a saddle, cut a piece of felt about 10 cm x 3 cm (4 in. x 1 ¼ in.), and round off the corners. Glue it across your horse's back. (You can glue on beads, sequins or rhinestones to decorate the saddle.)

5 For the mane, thread an arm's length of yarn in the large needle. Poke the needle in and bring it back out close by. Pull the yarn through and snip it, leaving yarn ends on both sides. Knot the ends together. Continue the mane down the neck.

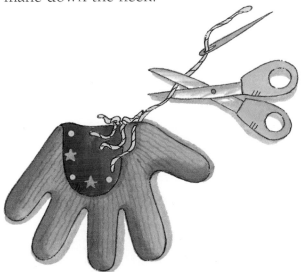

6 For the tail, use the needle to pull through three or four long pieces of yarn, one at a time. Tie them together with an overhand knot. Trim the tail.

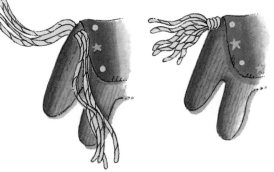

7 Cut two small felt triangle ears with rounded sides. Fold each ear in half and stitch each one in place.

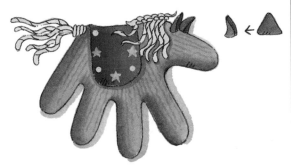

8 Use fabric paint to draw on nostrils and a mouth. Use roly eyes, paint or beads for the eyes. Tie a 25 cm (10 in.) length of cord or ribbon around the muzzle and knot the ends together for reins.

Beanbag starfish

*Try making this starfish with
shiny fabric on one side and
a plain fabric on the other.*

YOU WILL NEED

- a pencil, paper, thin cardboard, scissors
  and white craft glue
- 2 different pieces of fabric,
  each about 23 cm (9 in.) square
- a fabric marker or chalk pencil
- straight pins, a needle and thread
- beans or plastic pellets
- 2 pony beads
- dimensional fabric paint
  or permanent fabric markers
- an old stretchy, knit glove
  and a small pom-pom

1 Trace the starfish pattern from
page 36. Cut it out and glue it
onto the cardboard. Cut it out again.

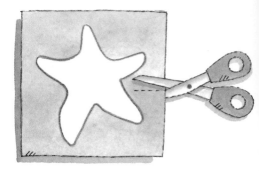

2 Trace the pattern on the wrong
side of the shiny fabric. Mark the
area to be left open.

3 Lay this fabric square over the
plain fabric so that the right sides
are together. Pin across your traced
lines and in the corners.

4 Backstitch (see page 7) along the traced line from one end of the area to be left open around to the other end. Remove the pins as you sew.

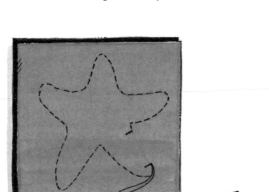

5 Cut out the starfish leaving about 0.5 cm (¼ in.) of fabric all around. Clip the seams in the corners and curves being careful not to cut your stitches.

6 Turn the starfish right side out. Use a closed pair of scissors to gently poke out the corners. Pour (or spoon) in the beans. Tuck in the raw edges and stitch the opening closed.

7 Glue on the pony-bead eyes. Use the permanent fabric markers or paint to draw on a face. Let it dry.

8 To make a hat, cut off a finger from the glove. Roll up the edge, glue on a pom-pom and stitch or glue it in place.

Beanbag frog

This frog can stretch out flat or sit up straight. Use wildly colorful printed fabric on one side and a plain matching fabric on the other.

YOU WILL NEED

- a pencil, paper, thin cardboard, scissors and white craft glue
- 2 different pieces of fabric, each about 30 cm x 25 cm (12 in. x 10 in.)
- a fabric marker or chalk pencil
- straight pins, a needle and thread
- beans or plastic pellets
- 2 small pom-poms
- 2 medium-sized roly eyes

1 Trace the frog pattern from page 37 and cut it out. Glue it onto the cardboard and cut it out again.

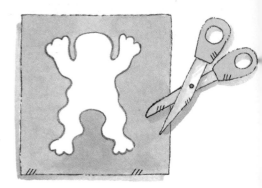

2 Trace the pattern on the wrong side of the plain fabric. Mark the area to be left open.

3 Lay this fabric over the printed one with the right sides together. Pin across your traced lines and in the corners.

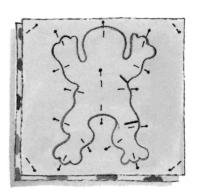

4 Backstitch (see page 7) along the traced line from one end of the area to be left open around to the other end. Remove the pins as you sew.

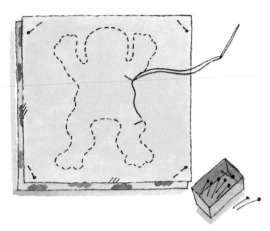

5 Cut out the frog leaving about 0.5 cm (¼ in.) of fabric all around. Clip the seams in the curves and toes, being careful not to cut your stitches.

6 Turn the frog right side out. Use a closed pair of scissors to poke out the toes. Pour (or spoon) beans into the opening. Tuck in the raw edges and stitch the opening closed.

7 Glue the pom-poms onto your frog's head. Glue the roly eyes onto the pom-poms.

OTHER IDEAS

• If you find it difficult to cut and sew the toes, trace the pattern but round the feet. When your frog is finished, use embroidery floss or a permanent marker to mark the toes.

• Give your frog a long red felt tongue. Stitch or glue it in place.

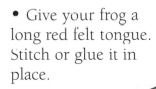

Beanbag ladybug

With sneakers on, this ladybug is really going places! Make it in two colors of Polarfleece or other thick, soft fabric.

YOU WILL NEED

- a pencil, paper, thin cardboard, scissors and white craft glue
- 1 red and 1 black 25 cm (10 in.) square of fabric
- a fabric marker or chalk pencil
- scraps of black felt or fleece
- straight pins, a needle and thread
- a pair of animal eyes (optional)
- stuffing and/or beans
- black dimensional fabric paint or a permanent fabric marker
- a needle and embroidery floss in black and white

1 Trace the ladybug and foot patterns from page 38 and cut them out. Glue them onto the cardboard and cut them out again.

2 Trace the ladybug pattern on the wrong side of each fabric square. Cut out both shapes. Mark the area to be left open on each one.

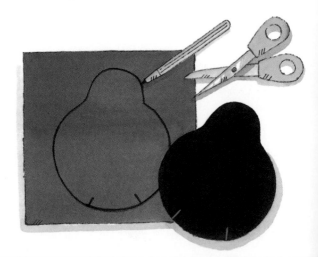

3 For the feet, trace and cut out the foot pattern six times from the black fleece. Pin the feet on the right side of the black ladybug shape so that the edges are even and the feet are pointing toward the head. (They should not be in the area to be left open.)

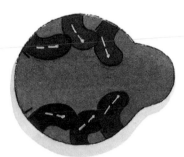

4 Carefully snip or poke two tiny holes for the eyes on the red shape. Push in the eyes and lock them in place with the back fasteners. (If you don't have animal eyes, draw eyes on with fabric paint at step 9.)

5 Pin the red shape right side down on top of the black one so the feet are covered.

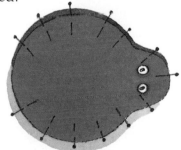

6 Backstitch (see page 7) from one end of the area to be left open around to the other end. Remove the pins as you sew.

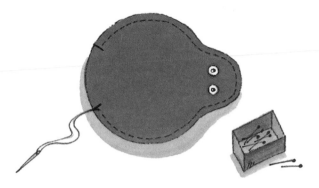

7 Clip the corners where the head and body meet and turn the ladybug right side out.

8 Stuff the head especially around the eye posts. Fill the rest of the ladybug with the beans. Tuck in the raw edges and stitch the opening closed. Turn the page to find out how to finish your ladybug.

Instructions continue on the next page ☞

9 Use the fabric marker or paint to draw a neck line and a line down the center of your ladybug's back. Draw on spots and a mouth. Allow the bug to dry.

10 For antennae, thread a piece of black embroidery floss through the needle. Make a knot at one end of the floss and another 2.5 cm (1 in.) from the end. Thread the floss through the head where you want one antenna and poke it out where you want the other. Make a third knot close to the head on this side and a fourth knot 2.5 cm (1 in.) farther away. Trim the floss. For thicker antennae, pull through, braid and knot three longer strands of floss.

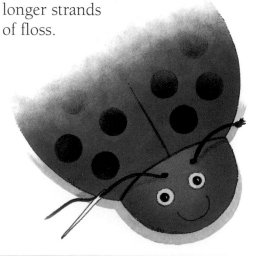

11 To make the antennae stand up, spread glue on them. Place the ladybug upside down, with its head over the edge of a table so the antennae hang down to dry.

12 For each shoelace, thread white floss through the ankle area and leave a tail about 10 cm (4 in.) long. Make three overcast stitches (see page 7) to the top part of the shoe and then cross them by making three stitches back. Cut the floss, leaving a 10 cm (4 in.) tail. Tie the tails into a bow. Trim the ends. Secure the bow and each lace end with a dab of glue.

Baby beanbag bug

You will need most of the same supplies as for the ladybug (see page 18).

1 Follow steps 1 and 2 on page 18 using the baby beanbag bug pattern on page 38.

2 With the right sides together, pin the two shapes. Backstitch or overcast stitch (see page 7) from one end of the area to be left open around to the other end. Remove the pins as you sew.

3 Turn the bug right side out. Fill it with the beans. Tuck in the raw edges and stitch the opening closed.

4 Use the fabric marker or paint to draw a neck line and another line down the center of your bug's back. Draw on spots and a face.

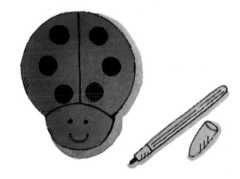

5 When the bug is dry, follow the instructions in step 10 on page 20 to make the antennae, but make them a little shorter.

Pocket puppy

This little pup is small enough to snuggle down in your pocket or pencil case. If you like, tie a bow or collar around its neck.

YOU WILL NEED

- a pencil, paper, thin cardboard, scissors and white craft glue
- a piece of fabric about 15 cm x 20 cm (6 in. x 8 in.)
- a fabric marker or chalk pencil
- straight pins, a needle and thread
- stuffing and/or beans
- scraps of felt
- decorating supplies (see step 8)

1 Trace the pattern from page 37 and cut it out. Glue it onto the cardboard and cut it out again.

2 Fold your fabric in half, right sides together. Pin it in the corners. Trace the pattern on the fabric.

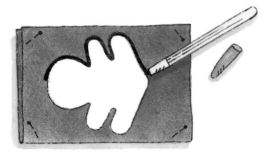

3 Backstitch (see page 7) along your traced line around until you get back to where you started. Make a couple of small stitches on the same spot and cut the thread.

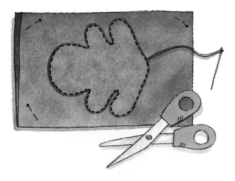

4 Remove the pins. Trim closely around the outside of the dog. Be careful not to cut any stitches.

5 Carefully make a cut about 4 cm (1 ½ in.) long down the center of your dog through one layer only. Turn it right side out. Use the eraser end of a pencil to push out the legs.

6 Stuff the legs first and then the rest of your puppy. Stitch the opening closed.

7 Cut out droopy felt ears and stitch or glue them on.

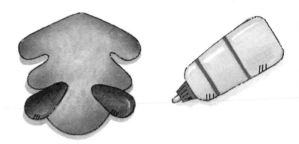

8 Glue on small beads or roly eyes and a tiny pom-pom or small bead for the nose. Or draw on the pup's face with a permanent fabric marker or paint. Draw or stitch on paws.

OTHER IDEAS

Make a pocket piglet using the puppy pattern. Curl a piece of pipe cleaner around a pencil and poke it into the tail area with a drop of glue. Give your piglet a two-hole button nose and draw on hooves.

Buttons bear

You can make this little bear out of almost any soft, thick fabric such as corduroy, Polarfleece or denim from old jeans.

YOU WILL NEED

- a pencil, paper, thin cardboard, scissors and white craft glue
- a piece of fabric about 40 cm x 50 cm (16 in. x 20 in.)
- a fabric marker or chalk pencil
- buttons   • an old sock
- straight pins, a needle and thread
- stuffing and beans
- permanent fabric marker or dimensional fabric paint

1 Trace the bear pattern from page 39 and cut it out. Glue it onto the cardboard and cut it out again.

2 Trace the bear pattern twice on the wrong side of your fabric. Cut both bear shapes out. Mark the area to be left open on one of the bear shapes.

3 Stitch on the button eyes and nose.

4 Pin the bear pieces with right sides together. Backstitch (see page 7) them together, leaving the marked area open. Remove all the pins. Clip the curves and corners.

5 Turn the bear right side out. Use stuffing in the head and limbs. Pour (or spoon) beans into the rest of the body. Tuck in the edges and overcast stitch (see page 7) the opening closed.

6 For the vest, cut off about 9 cm (3½ in.) of ribbing from the sock. Cut slits 4 cm (1½ in.) long on each side about 2 cm (¾ in.) down from the top.

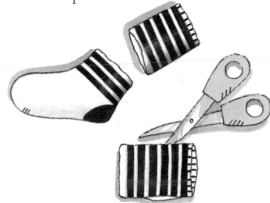

7 Sew two or more buttons down the front. Slide the vest onto the bear. Roll down the neck and turn under the bottom.

8 Use the markers or paint to finish the face. You can also add paws and claws.

Baby chick

*This little chick looks cute tucked
into its soft shell. Make many of
these in lots of bright colors.*

YOU WILL NEED

- a pencil, paper, thin cardboard, scissors
  and white craft glue
- a square of felt
- a fabric marker or chalk pencil
- straight pins, a needle and thread
- a piece of fabric about 10 cm x 14 cm
  (4 in. x 5 ½ in.)
- stuffing or beans
- a short piece of narrow ribbon
- a piece of gathered lace about 10 cm
  (4 in.) long
- embroidery floss
- a small two-hole button
- decorating supplies (see step 7)

1 Trace the eggshell pattern from
page 36 and cut it out. Glue it
onto the cardboard and cut it out again.
Trace it onto the felt twice. Cut out
both pieces.

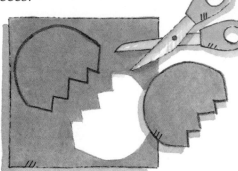

2 Pin the shells together. Backstitch
or overcast stitch (see page 7)
them together. Remove the pins. Turn
the shell right side out. Set it aside.

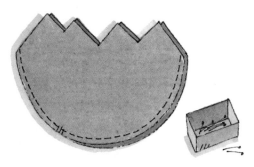

3 Fold and pin the rectangle of
fabric in half, right sides together.
Backstitch (see page 7) down from the
top and up from the bottom, leaving
the center area open.

4 Use doubled thread to sew a running stitch about 0.5 cm (¼ in.) from the top all the way around. Pull on the thread and wrap it a couple of times around the gathered area. Make a few stitches in one spot to hold the gathers. Repeat this for the bottom.

5 Turn the chick right side out. Stuff it and stitch it closed. The stitched area should be at the back of your chick.

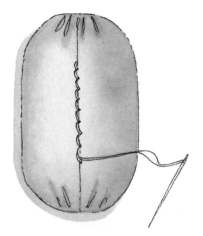

6 Tie the ribbon around the chick's neck. Knot it at the back and trim the ends. Dab glue on the knot to secure it.

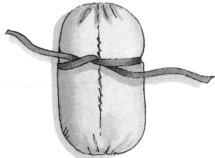

7 Stitch or glue the gathered lace around the chick's head. Trim the ends. Draw or glue on eyes.

8 For a soother, make an overhand knot near the looped end of a doubled piece of embroidery floss. Thread a floss end through each hole of the button and knot the ends on the other side. Trim the floss. Glue the soother in place, holding it until it begins to dry.

Sock bunny

This bunny will jump out in style if you use a sock with different-colored toe and heel areas. For the sweater, you can use an old, holey sock as long as the ribbing is in good shape.

YOU WILL NEED

- a needle and thread
- 2 adult-sized socks in different colors
- a ruler, scissors and glue • stuffing
- 2 medium-sized two-hole buttons
- a dollmaker's needle (long and strong)
- decorating supplies (see step 10)
- 1 small and 1 medium pom-pom
- thin craft wire

1 Knot a doubled length of thread in your needle. Sew a running stitch through both layers, across the width of the sock about 8 cm (3 in.) from the toe. Pull on the thread to gather the area together. Make a few stitches in the same spot to hold the gathers. Trim the thread.

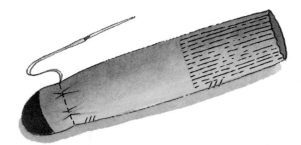

2 For ears, cut down the center of the sock from the toe to the stitching. Tuck in the raw edges and overcast stitch (see page 7) each ear closed.

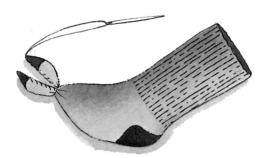

3 Stuff the foot of the sock from the ears to the heel.

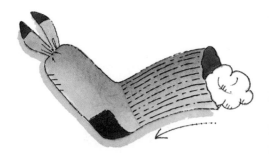

4 Cut off and set aside part of the ribbing, leaving enough ribbing to make legs. Cut this leg area down the center. Overcast stitch (see page 7) the side of each leg. Stuff the legs and stitch them closed.

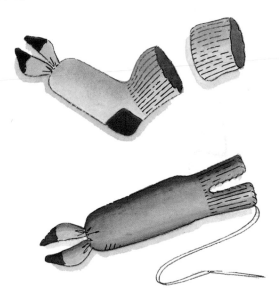

5 Cut a piece of thread about 60 cm (24 in.) long and double it. Tie it around the neck. Triple knot the thread and trim it.

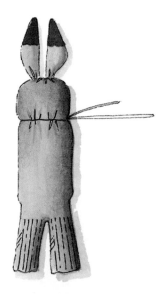

6 Cut off about 10 cm (4 in.) of ribbing from the other sock. Slide this onto your bunny. Roll down the top of the ribbing. Make sure it covers the neck thread. Tuck under the raw edges at the bottom of the sweater.

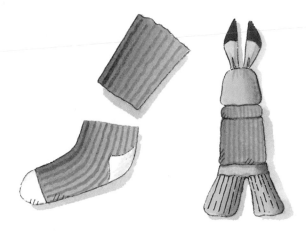

7 From the set-aside ribbing, cut two arm pieces, each about 10 cm x 8 cm (4 in. x 3 in.). Fold them in half lengthwise with the right sides together. Backstitch or overcast stitch (see page 7) each of them along one end and one side. Turn them right side out, stuff them and stitch them closed.

Instructions continue on the next page ☞

8 To fasten on the arms, knot doubled thread into the dollmaker's needle. Poke the needle in one shoulder and through the body so the tip is sticking out the other side. Push one arm onto the needle and draw the needle and thread through the arm. Thread on a button and push the needle back through the other button hole, arm and body to the other shoulder.

9 Push the other arm onto the tip of the needle, pull the needle through and thread on the other button. Continue back and forth until the arms are well fastened. Make a couple of small stitches under one of the arms, knot the thread and trim it.

10 Use roly eyes, beads, felt or fabric paint to make eyes, a mouth and, if you wish, teeth. Glue on the small pom-pom for the nose and the larger one for the tail.

11 To make glasses, cut a piece of wire about 20 cm (8 in.) long. Make a circle near the center of the wire by wrapping it around a pen or pencil and twisting it three times. Make another circle close by in the same way. Both wire ends will be in the center area. Wind the ends around the wire frames and position them to look like the arms of the glasses. Trim the arms if necessary and poke them in at each side of the bunny's eyes to hold the glasses in place.

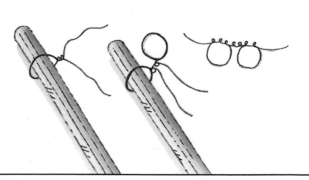

Sock lion

Here's another great way to recycle an old sock into a new friend.

YOU WILL NEED

- 1 or 2 adult-sized socks
- scissors and a ruler
- a yarn needle and yarn
- stuffing • scraps of felt
- a needle and thread
- decorating supplies (see step 9)

1 Turn the sock inside out. Cut a piece above the heel that is 15 cm to 20 cm (6 in. to 8 in.) long. Set aside the foot.

2 With the needle and yarn, sew a row of running stitches around one end of the sock, 1 cm (½ in.) from the edge. Leave a yarn tail at the start and finish. Pull the yarn out of the needle and pull on both ends to gather the sock closed. Double knot the ends. Repeat this for the other end of the sock.

Instructions continue on the next page ☞

3 Cut a lengthwise slit in the sock and turn the sock right side out. Stuff it and overcast stitch (see page 7) the opening closed. This should be the underside of your lion.

4 For the legs, cut out four 8 cm (3 in.) squares from the foot of the sock or from another sock. Fold each one in half, right sides together. Backstitch (see page 7) each one along one side and one end. Turn them right side out, stuff them and stitch them closed.

5 One end of your sock tube will be the head. Stitch or glue the legs onto the lion so that the front legs extend past the head. The lion will look like it's resting on its paws.

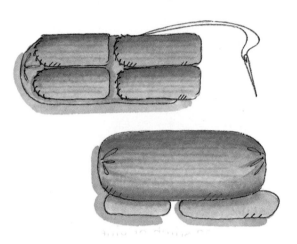

6 For the mane, thread yarn into the needle and pull the ends even. Poke the needle in near the face area and bring it back out close by. Pull the yarn through and snip it, leaving yarn ends on both sides. Knot these ends together. Continue around the face. Untwist each piece of yarn and separate the strands. Trim the mane.

7 For the tail, use the needle to pull through three lengths of yarn, one at a time, so you have six strands. Braid the strands, knot them and unravel the end bits. Trim the yarn if necessary.

8 Cut two small, rounded ears out of felt. Pinch together the bottom of each ear and stitch or glue each one to the lion's head.

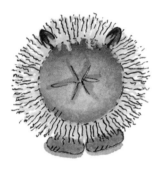

9 Use roly eyes, buttons, beads, felt scraps, permanent fabric markers, paint or yarn for the face. Draw on claws if you wish.

OTHER IDEAS

• For a crown, glue gold or silver foil on thin cardboard. Cut out a crown shape. Glue on sequins or rhinestones. Glue, tape or staple it together and crown your king of the jungle.

• Try making a sock elephant. Give it big, felt ears. For the trunk, cut a long rectangle from a scrap of sock and sew it into a tube. Stitch it in place. For the legs, cut out four circles from sock scraps and run a line of stitches around the outside of each. Gather, stuff and stitch each in place.

• What other animals can you make? Try a rhinoceros, hippopotamus or a smaller animal such as a beaver or a guinea pig.

33

Cool cat

*For this cat, use wild-animal print fabric.
Or make a tame cat by using plain fabric.
If you wish to use specially made cat eyes,
follow step 4 on page 19.*

YOU WILL NEED

• a pencil, paper, ruler, thin cardboard,
scissors, and white craft glue

• about 0.3 m (⅓ yd.) of fabric

• a fabric marker or chalk pencil

• straight pins, a needle and thread

• stuffing

• permanent fabric markers
or dimensional fabric paint

• a strip of felt or Polarfleece

1 Trace the patterns for the paws,
head and body from page 40.
Cut them out. Tape the head and
body pattern pieces together along the
dotted lines. Glue the patterns onto
the cardboard and cut them out again.

2 Trace the head and body pattern
twice onto the fabric and the
paws eight times. Cut out all ten pieces.
On one of the head and body pieces,
mark the area to be left open.

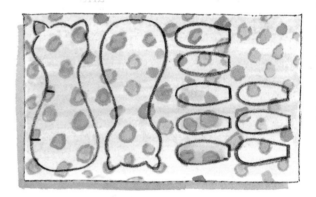

3 For the tail, cut a strip of fabric
9 cm x 45 cm (3 ½ in. x 18 in.)
long. Fold it in half lengthwise, right
sides together. Pin and stitch it along
one end and the long side.

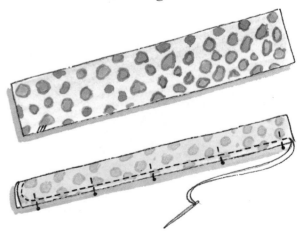

4 Pin and backstitch (see page 7) the right sides of the head and body pieces together, except for the area to be left open. Stitch about 0.5 cm (¼ in.) in from the edges.

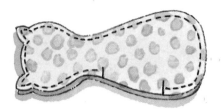

5 Pair the paws and pin and backstitch them together. Leave all the tops open.

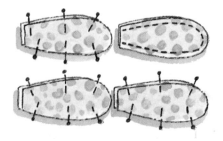

6 Remove all the pins. Clip the curves, being careful not to snip your stitches. Turn all six cat parts right side out using a wooden spoon.

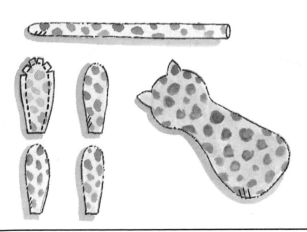

7 Stuff the body, paws and tail, using a spoon to push in the stuffing. Stitch each part closed.

8 Stitch the paws to the body so they hang loosely. Stitch on the tail.

9 Draw the face with fabric markers or dimensional fabric paint.

10 Make a scarf by cutting a strip of felt or fleece about 60 cm x 8 cm (24 in. x 3 in.). Cut a fringe and tie it around the cat's neck.

Patterns

Baby chick shell
from page 26

Beanbag starfish from page 14

leave open

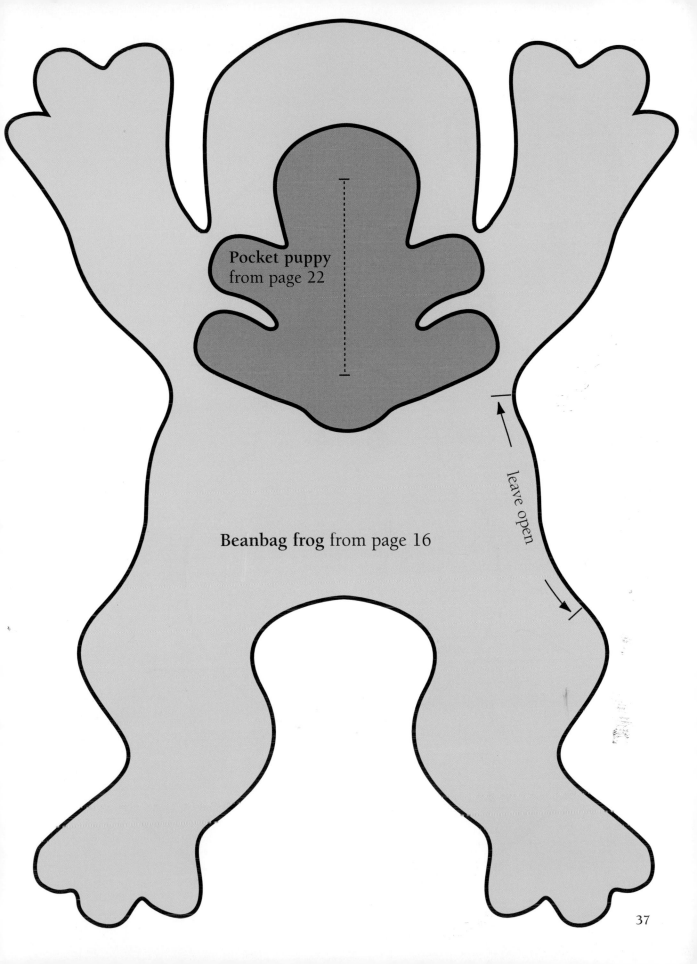

Pocket puppy
from page 22

Beanbag frog from page 16

leave open

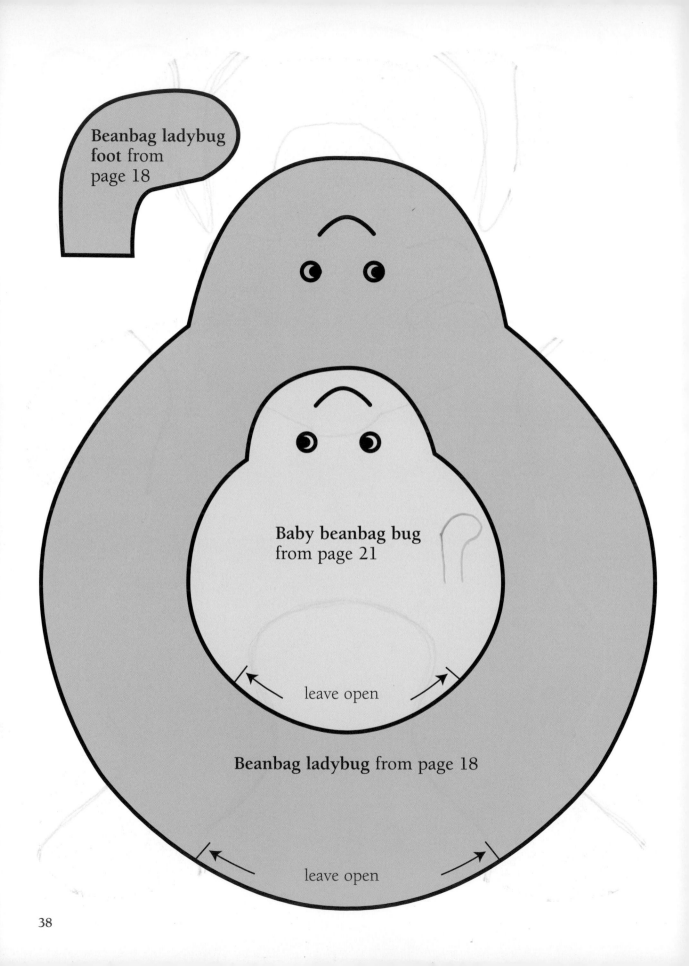

Beanbag ladybug foot from page 18

Baby beanbag bug from page 21

leave open

Beanbag ladybug from page 18

leave open

Buttons bear from page 24

leave open

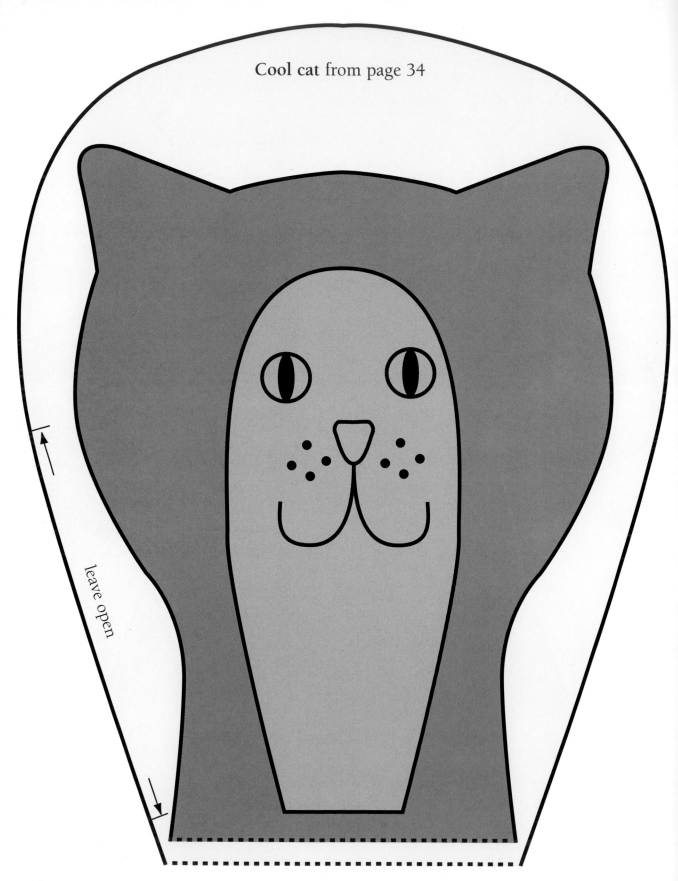

Cool cat from page 34

leave open